Kindness Is the Most Powerful
Little Thing
in the World

Three Types of Transformational Kindness for Everyone

By Bryan Lee Martin

Dedication

To Joanna, a freaking amazing miracle of astronomical proportions.

Contents

Introduction

Quick! Think of the kindest person you ever met, someone you actually knew. Got it? Okay, now what did that person actually do to demonstrate kindness? What was it about that person that was so kind? Did that person smile at you? Did that person say nice things to you? Was that person there for you? Did that person send you notes and cards? Did that person give you special gifts? Did that person think that you were special? The answer is undoubtedly "Yes" to most of these questions and more. Please note that all these things are actually little things, things anyone can do at just about any time. They didn't take much effort, time or energy to perform. Nevertheless, they were so special to you that you remember them to this day. Their kindness transformed you from being an ordinary person into being a special human being. You were recognized, validated, accepted, appreciated, honored, respected, and most of all loved. Wow! All that by a little thing called kindness.

Now let's go to a place that might be uncomfortable for you to think about. Let's go to your funeral. Pretend I am the ghost of "That which is yet to come," but I am kind and not mean and you feel safe with me. Here... hold my hand. As you look around you recognize most of the people at your funeral. They are your friends and family, the ones you love and care for the most. One of them stands up and uses your pet name. Here I'm going to use the name "Fufu" but when you read Fufu you will read and hear the name people call you.

"Fufu, was one of the most important people in my life! (there is a brief emotional pause) I would not be the person I am today without Fufu's love. I remember a time when I thought my world was coming to an end when out of nowhere I got a letter in the mail from Fufu. It was brief but in it Fufu told me about the love Fufu had for me and how much Fufu wanted to hug me and kiss me. At that time I couldn't imagine anyone wanting to hug and kiss me. Fufu didn't know all that I was going through and that letter came at just the right time. I still have that letter. I will never forget Fufu's smile. When Fufu smiled at you Fufu's entire face lit up. I could feel Fufu's smile deep in my belly. I knew peace more when Fufu smiled than any other time. Fufu did a lot of great things in the world. Fufu was a great business person, served important roles in the community, and did little quirky things that people always talked about. But the most important and lasting thing Fufu ever did was the kindness and love Fufu showed in all the little things Fufu did for us. None of us will ever be the same, all are better because of Fufu. Fufu will always live big in our hearts and we will always tell our friends and grandkids of Fufu's love and kindness."

Let me bring you back, now, to this little book about kindness. Your funeral gives you a little picture of your life. It shows you some very important things about you. It shows you the impact you have on other people. It shows you that your life is more meaningful than you ever realized. Your funeral shows you that the love and kindness you show is far greater than any of your achievements, your career, and the amount of money you might make. In the end your loving kindness, revealed in the little things you do, is the most important aspect of your being.

That is why it is so important to constantly be learning about love and kindness. As important as kindness is there are very few places to learn about it. In fact, I'll bet that you can't name more than a few places that are fully dedicated to teaching kindness. Not your home. You learned a lot of good things at home but it was not dedicated totally to kindness. Not your religion. Religion taught you about religious and spiritual things, rituals, beliefs, and love including some about kindness, but religion is not 100% about kindness. How you learned about kindness is that you picked up pieces here and there from people's examples, some from home, some from religion, some from watching Mr. Rogers and media like that. Very few people attend a course totally about kindness. Yet loving kindness is one of the most important transformational little things in human life, if not the most important.

So I would like to welcome you and congratulate you for reading, taking a little course on kindness. By attending your own funeral you have seen how important kindness is. But that is just the beginning of the importance of kindness. Kindness is the cure for all the unkindness in the world.

Meanness and unkindness is everywhere in the world, from the home, the playground and in the shopping center parking lot. You will find meanness in the nations' capitals, on all types of media and international business. How meanness got there is the content of another book. What's important is that we, you and I, can make a significant impact on the world just by being more intentional with our loving kindness. If you and I make a pledge to eliminate all negativity from our thoughts, words and actions… if we pledge to be kind 100% of the time and when we aren't we take back control of our thoughts, words and actions to be kind again, think about how our world and our lives would be better.

I know. It is a crazy thought to think we can live a 100% kind life, that we can change the world with kindness. Crazy or not let's give it a try. I take that back. Let's not try. Let's do it!

I have divided this book into two parts. Part One is all about the kindness mindset. it begins with understanding what a "thought" is. That is so important for you to know. Because when you know what a thought is then you can control your thoughts, your feelings, your emotions, and your actions. You CAN control your thoughts, you know!

Once you learn how to control your thoughts I will show you how you can use your System Two thinking process to help you control your thoughts even better (Don't worry I will explain System Two and System One thoughts).

Next I will show you two types of thoughts you can have about human beings. It is so important that you know just how amazing people are, including you.

Lastly in Part One I will share with you the necessity of doing little thing and being kind from a loving heart. We don't do loving things expecting to get something in return. There is benefit in being kind. But that's not the point. The point is changing the world with kindness.

Part Two consist of understanding the three types of kindness. I will show you how you can have kind thoughts 100% of the time! Next we discuss the incredible power of your kind words. Then we will spend some time going over a million ways that you can do kind acts. Well… if not a million then at least we will make a good start. After that I will share strategies for teaching kids kindness. Finally, I will ask you to adopt the Kindness Statement as your own commitment to live a kind life. That may be the greatest kind act you will ever make! And this may be the most important book you will ever read!

And here is some more good news. This is the first book in a series on love. L.O.V.E. is an acronym I use to describe and teach about love. "L" is for little things. There are three types of little things, kind thoughts, kind words and kind actions. That is what this book is about. "O" stands for Oxytocin, the hug drug, and is a metaphor for developing emotional closeness in relationships. Would you like to experience greater emotional connections with your people? I thought so. "V" is for Victory and stand for being victorious in problem solving at home and in the world. I'll bet you have had a few problems in life and would like a few tips about how to solve them better with less drama and emotion. "E" stand for Eternity which is a metaphor for having meaning and significance in life. I am working on the "E" book next.

Doesn't that sound great! I am so excited to share these ideas with you.

For now, let us focus our attention on kindness. In L.O.V.E. the most obvious manifestation of love is little things like kind thoughts, kind words, and kind acts. I am thinking kind thoughts about you as you read this book. May it be a blessing in your life.

Part One
The Kindness Mindset

The word "mindset" is used in many domains like education, professional sports and business. In business training programs some trainers say success is 90% mindset and 10% skill. That means that one can be more skilled and better trained than others but if the mindset is off then less skillful people with a different mindset will be more successful.

Mindset is how you approach your business or your life. It is your basic assumptions. There are many metaphors for mindset like your psychology, or your basic operating system, and your world view. Mindset is general concepts or thinking systems which are organizing principles. For many they are mostly unconscious. People get their mindset from what is caught and taught in their growing up environment, at school, or in the prevailing culture in which they live. Perhaps the sub-culture you identify with the most has the most influence over your mindset. There are three sub-cultures which have affected my mindset as an adult. The first is my religious culture. I was immersed in the evangelical/neo-Pentecostal movement of the early 1970s in southern California and was trained in evangelical theological institutions. That was an extremely powerful influence! The second sub-culture that influenced me was my education and training as a marriage and family counselor and psychotherapist. That was profound! The third sub-culture has been the business training I received in the context of our real estate businesses. The real estate franchise which we affiliated with has been recognized as a premier training and consulting business and has a well-defined culture. I am thankful for all the different learning opportunities and experiences from these cultures.

Over the years I learned how to understand the basic assumptions and tenets of these sub-cultures and the mindsets they instilled in me. Some aspects of these sub-culture and their contribution to my mindset I have continued to embrace and others I moved away from. For instance, I have moved away from the idea that people are basically and fundamentally flawed and require being fixed or cured. Now I embrace the idea that human beings are "freaking amazing miracles of astronomical proportions" who are "endowed with or have developed gifts, skills talents and tool to benefit themselves and others." The only intervention most people need is information, education, inspiration, encouragement and empowerment. I must tell you that from where I have come this is a huge leap. One aspect of my religious sub-culture that I continue to embrace is the supreme importance of love. Love really is the most important thing. I have given a lot of thought about how my mindset has been shaped. My mindset is revealed in this book. I hope that as you read this you are wondering about your mindset and how it came to be.

Carol Dweck, author of "Mindset" states that there is a growth mindset and a fixed mindset. My experience is that the more aware one is, as people learn more about their self, as they give more thought to their processes, they can control and develop their mindset. But learning is just one way to influence your mindset. Mindset is also affected by life experience. When one experiences the kindness of a helper, like a teacher or a health professional, it can spur them on to become a helper, too, like them. Your mindset is also influenced by the things you do habitually, especially rituals. During the holiday season you engage in holiday rituals and you become more intentional in your thoughts and actions in many domains such as cooking special meals, attending special gatherings, sharing gifts, participating in religious events. Your mindset is stimulated by your activities. Intentionally engaging in activities affects your mindset.

This discussion is important because kindness has a particular mindset. You are endowed with kindness because you are a human being. But you can enhance your kindness and raise it to a higher and more prominent place in your thinking by learning, experiencing, doing, and being more intentional about kindness; by having a kindness mindset. The benefits of having an elevated awareness, increased intentionality and purposeful kindness for you and others is greater than you can imagine. Moreover, the impact of your kindness can impact and help future generations. So let us take some time to help grow a kindness mindset.

Chapter 1
How You Think

Kindness begins with how you think. This seems to be the most obvious point, right? But here is what I discovered, that people are largely unaware of their thought processes. In fact, if you were to do a random survey and ask people, "What is a thought?" they would be hard pressed to give you an answer. Is it an idea that pops in your head? Is it created by the devil or by the Lord? I think you will be surprised at the answer.

A thought is the biological process of neurons, chemicals and electric impulses in your brain. That's it, bada bing bada boom, drop the mic. Yes, there are billions of neurons and trillions of electric impulses in that chemical bathtub called your brain. All these connections make for a dynamic biological process of which there is nothing else like on earth (and maybe in the Universe!). But it is really not much different than the way you eat your food. You put food in your mouth, you chew it up and it goes into your stomach where it is broken down into tiny units as it passes through your small and large intestine. The good stuff is spun off as nutrients and carried to parts of your body to feed cells and the bad stuff, waste and gas find their way out of your body. Thoughts are systematic formulations of neurons sending and receiving messages to various parts of the brain finding learned memories and organizing them at the speed of light so that your food taste savory or sweet, the flower is beautiful, her death makes you feel sad, you need to step over that pile of poop on the lawn, and following the plans you can build a house, bridge, or space traveling rockets. Literally every thought you have is a biological process and (this may be the most important thing you ever learn) you have control over your thoughts. Let me explain.

You remember how you process food? The food goes in and waste and gas comes out. Imagine you are in the grocery store shopping for more food. As you walk down the frozen food aisle you realize that it is time for some of that gas to, you know, get out. You look down the aisle and there is a young mother with her three little kid and you don't want to "make a scene" so you hold it and walk around the corner to the next aisle where there is no one and you pause, move your body just right and let it go. I know you are laughing out loud now because you know exactly what I'm talking about and you have done it yourself! What you did was that you controlled the process. That gas had to go and you controlled when and where. Well, here is the good news. You can control your thoughts, too!

We all have brain farts and, believe it or not, we can control our stinking thinking. I discovered this one night at 3:00 am. I woke up, thinking about a real estate transaction going bad at the last minute leaving my client with a truck load of all their worldly possession parked outside the home they thought they were buying and, worse, the prospect of maybe not having a home at all! My heart was pounding in my chest 90 miles an hour. "OH MY GOD! What am I going to do? Then I stopped myself Jerry Seinfeld style... "What a minute! It's 3:00 am! I can't do anything about this at 3:00 am. Besides, I have had worse problems than this. It's just a problem and everything will work out. I am not going to think about this. There must be a million things I can think about besides this transaction." Sure enough I started thinking about a talk I was looking forward to giving in a few days. I organized it into its parts and added a few funny stories. Amazingly in a few moments my heart slowed so did my breathing and the next thing I knew the alarm was going off. My discovery about controlling my thoughts is not new. People have been controlling their thoughts for thousands of years. What's new is the discovery of brain function. A thought is merely brain function and we have tremendous control over what we think.

Feelings and emotions are also the biological processes of the human brain. They are neurons, electrical impulses and chemicals. All of your sadness, all of your happiness, all of your fear and all of your anger are reactions formulated in your brain in response to specific situations AND you can control them.

You have probably read, heard or know that fear and anxiety are associated with the chemical adrenaline which is part of your "Fight or Flee" response. That ancient response was built into you to keep you safe from saber toothed tigers. It gives you what seems like super human power to run like heck or fight for your life in threatening situations. That's good, right? The problem is that you don't need a superhuman adrenaline rush when you get into an argument with your spouse or your kid. Yet the old Fight or Flee shows up today at home in the middle of your argument as if you were fighting for your life. If your throat is sore from screaming and there are holes in the wall after your argument chance are you had a little adrenaline rush. You can control that. It takes some work but you can control it. I assure you that you don't need an adrenaline rush to solve domestic problems, or frustrating problems. So here is how you control it.

It begins with being aware of your body. You can tell when you are angry. Stop and check out what is happening in your body. If your heart rate is higher that 100 beats per minute that is a sure sign that you have adrenaline coursing through your veins. Your brain and body is officially flooded with the powerful drug adrenaline! You can control it but it will not stop instantly. It may take an hour or longer for your liver to process the adrenaline sufficiently. Here is how you can know when you are not flooded any more, when your pulse rate returns to the baseline level of around 70 beats per minute. Since it takes a while the only way to control your bodies continued release of adrenaline is to get away from the stimulus. That means leave the argument. This is not so easy because a further effect of the adrenaline is that it makes the argument seem urgent, as if it were a life or death situation. Only it is not life or death. It is just an argument. Here is an interesting fact I have discovered from personal experience and from working with couples; frequently couples can't remember what they were arguing about hours or even minutes after the argument. The adrenaline has the effect of making the argument intensely important. So it is important to leave the argument even if it seems like the problem needs to be taken care of now. Just leave. Leaving is controlling. Here is one way to leave the argument. Say this: "I am so upset I feel sick. I have to leave now! When I feel better we can figure this out. I will come back when I feel better." When you leave you will need to turn your attention to something else. If you keep ruminating about the argument you may find yourself exciting your Fight or Flee response and perpetuate the adrenaline rush. It could take several hours to escape the cycle.

There are other ways to combat the negative effects of the chemical rush. Deep breathing is extremely effective. It is a good idea to learn deep breathing techniques just for good health. Deep breathing will activate your parasympathetic response, also known as the "relaxation response." The relaxation response will send other chemicals through your body to counteract the effect of negative chemicals. So when you breathe deeply you are taking back control.

I need to add here that if your domestic disputes cause frequent releases of adrenaline resulting in heated arguments then you can take control by getting some help from a counselling professional. Getting help from others is getting more control.

It is extremely important to gain more control in your life. So, please let me reiterate it one more time. All your thoughts, all your emotions and all of your feelings are the product of brain cells, electric impulses and chemicals. Everything, fear, anger, sadness, grief, happiness, surprise, disgust and every thought you have are all brain/body processes and you have control, more control that you ever imagined!

There is a long list of things you can do to control your mind and body in addition to getting away from stressor and deep breathing, things like, good sleeping habits, plenty of movement and exercise, being an active part of a community, connecting with friends, getting lot of sunshine, walking barefoot to ground yourself, having a mentor, coach, accountability partner, singing, playing an instrument, eating right, controlling your alcohol intake, helping other people, sustained focused attention (meditation, prayer and the like) hobbies, and belly laughing. There are more. Oh yes, you read it right, belling laughing.

When you come to Jennifer and my "Our Real Love" workshop I will demonstrate a belly laugh and get you to do one too. Talk about controlling your thinking! The rush of oxygen and the endorphins produced in a belly laugh are immediately noticeable and have a lingering effect. It is a good demonstration of how to control your thoughts. Here is some good news; you can learn how to control your thoughts for the rest of your life and your life will be better than you ever imagined. Let's turn our attention to System One and System Two thinking in preparation for learning how to think about people. Then we can take a deeper look into kindness.

Chapter 2
Systems One and Two Thoughts

Researchers have determined that there are two types of thoughts, System One and System Two thoughts. I learned about System One and System Two in "Thinking, Fast and Slow," by Nobel laureate Daniel Kahneman. I extend the metaphor to personal relationships. System One thoughts are the almost automatic thoughts that come to mind. When I ask you "What is one plus one?" even before the word "Two!" is formed on your lips it is in your mind. A vast majority of your thoughts are instantaneous thoughts which just seem to be effortlessly there.

System Two thoughts are the ones that require more effort and time to process. The classic example of System Two thinking is the bat and ball equation. See if you can figure this out. A bat and a ball cost $1.10 total. If the bat costs $1.00 more than the ball how much does the ball cost? Many people using System One thinking would say the ball cost 10 cents, and they would be wrong. Let me explain. If the ball cost 10 cents and the bat cost a dollar more ($1 more than 10 cents is $1.10) then the total would be $1.20. 10 cents plus $1.10 is $1.20 not $1.10. So the equation requires more thought. The correct answer is that the ball cost 5 cents and the bat cost $1.05 for a total of $1.10. System Two thinking requires more time and effort.

Love and kindness are System Two processes. They require more effort and time when thinking about people and relationships. When you meet a stranger you have an almost instantaneous response. "He is not creepy or dangerous looking, he appears to be friendly and approachable." This is a System One response. It happens instantly, almost without a thought. It is merely an initial assessment based on very basic information and perhaps the beginning of a relationship. Later on, perhaps during a dating or courting process, other System Two thinking kicks in and characteristics like emotional stability, kindness, dependability, great job history are evaluated prior to any kind of a continuing or long term relationship. Attraction and passion are System One processes. Determining if the other is a good fit as a long term partner requires more work, evaluation and analysis, System Two processes.

Here is another System One, System Two example. Has this ever happened to you? You and your spouse are at dinner with another couple when something is said in jest at your expense and your partner throws you under the bus, is demeaning, critical and sarcastic, yet in a humorous way. Nevertheless, your partner puts you down, out of nowhere, in front of the others and you are the butt of the joke. You laugh, too, but on the inside you are hurt, humiliated and you want to kill your partner, metaphorically of course. On the way home you confront your partner, have a huge argument.

You think, "Well if that is the way she/he thinks about me then we are done!" System One thinking responds instantly to the put down with hurt, anger and puts a big wall up. System One thinking makes you the victim. System One thinking makes it all about you and your safety. Personal safety is, after all, of the most importance in a relationship.

On the other hand, System Two thinking is more like Jerry Seinfeld and says "Hey...wait a minute! This really is not about me! She/he made the statement. What's going on that would make the other need to put me down?" It takes more work to think like this. Upon reflection it is obvious the need to put someone down is driven by some inferior feeling or thought, or something completely unknown inside the one who made the statement. So the work of System Two response is "Something may be wrong with the other. This is not what I expected from the other. I need to stay curious and figure this out." There is a vast difference between System One thinking and System Two thinking in relationships and love. Yes, it takes more time and effort to engage System Two thinking. You can see the problem is controlling the thinking process. System One has less control over thoughts, System Two works harder at controlling thoughts. Passion is easy, love and kindness require more thought control. This is something you and I can grow in.

Chapter 3
Two Thoughts You Can Have About People

There are two thoughts you can have about people. One is that people are fundamentally flawed and need intervention to help them. The other is that people are amazing and have innate and developed gifts, skills, talents and tools to help their self and the world. I belong to the second camp. When I was trained as a psychotherapist I was forced to think about people in the flawed and needing intervention camp. You see in order to get paid I had to label people with a diagnosis so I was forced to look for something wrong with them and develop a treatment plan for it. However most the people I saw would have done well simply by eliminating certain behaviors, focusing on building their strength areas and talking through their situations. I could help a couple struggling in their relationship by teaching them the dynamics of family life, how to repair damage, increase their emotional connection and throw in a crash course on financial management with empathy, love and listening. They didn't need a label, they needed education, encouragement and inspiration. I'm not suggesting that people don't need therapy. I am saying that seeing people as basically flawed has crept into our culture in a major way and that view misses one of the most amazing, wonderful and powerful aspect of the entire universe, that human beings are the most creative, loving, caring, innovative, thoughtful wonders in existence.

Some people will try to challenge me on this saying that the evil perpetrated by people proves that people are basically flawed. I'm not disagreeing that there are evil people in the world. I read history and the news too. But they are a very very small percentage and yet they have very very awful effects. Let's say one percent of the world's nearly 8 billion people is evil. That is a huge army of 800,000 people with evil intent! If they wanted to the one percent could destroy the earth! So I get that evil is real and a present problem in the world today. But that does not change my view about the 99% and the essential nature of humanity. Most people grow up in loving homes where parents struggle for the survival of the family because they love them and they want their children and grandchildren to survive, thrive and have a better life than the parents. Most homes want to build on their children's gifts, skills, talents and tools for their benefit and for the benefit of the world. It is my opinion that people are amazing miracles of astronomical proportions endowed with and developing gifts, skills, talents, and tools for their benefit and for the benefit of the world.

This affects the way I respond to people. Because I believe and think that people are amazing it is my intention to honor, dignify, and respect every person I encounter all the time and under nearly every circumstance. Isn't that a different way to think about people? Since each one is endowed with or has developed their own set of gifts, skills, talents and tools I am curious about what differentiates them and I want to learn from them. If they are seeking me out because they recognize my gifts, skills, talents, and tools I am honored by their inquiry and respond with my full attention.

Since I used the word "differentiate" I want to elaborate about it. I use to want to be an Outlier. I read Malcolm Gladwell's book and I thought how great would that be to be an Outlier. I came to realize that being an Outlier was very similar to the idea of being an individual. An individual is one who is set apart from the others. I have never been very successful at being an individual. I like being a part of my family, my school, my community. My experience was that being an individual was lonely. My identity was shaped more by my people, my relationships with them and my culture than by any individual aspect of my being. Then I thought about differentiation. The key difference between individuating and differentiating is that individuals stand alone and those who differentiate stand in the midst of their community. Even identical twins have aspects which differentiate them. And so it is in home, and schools, and communities, the work world, culture and society in general. People are differentiated by their innate and developed gifts, skills, talents, and tools. What differentiates us is, of course, that which is different. My gifts, skills, talents, and tools, such as they are, are somewhat unique to me. When I use my gifts, skills, talents and tools I differentiate myself from Terry, who as a brain surgeon is differentiated in my community by Terry's set of gifts, skills, talents and tools. Lauren, who is the owner of the grocery store, has Lauren's set. As I said, my set is different, I inspire, encourage, equip and teach people about love. Over the years I have come to view myself as differentiated standing with people rather than individuated, standing by myself.

When you think about it you will be able to come up with your own set of differentiating characteristics. Everyone has a set of gifts, skills, talents and tools. I am, you are, part of a home, community, team, construction crew, school, and so on. We all use our gifts, skills, talents, and tools for our own benefit (Benefits like having a sense of personhood and identity and for the monetary benefit of using those gifts) and for the benefit of others, as in caring for the unhealthy, keeping the public safe, creating commerce and exchange, and so on. It is by using our gifts, skills, talents, and tools that the world becomes better and better. Isn't differentiating a lovely way to think about people?

Here is a fun exercise to help you focus your thinking, or to say it in another way, how to control your thinking about others and yourself. Take note and pay attention to the people around you. People are a beautiful part of nature! So as you would appreciate a walk through Yosemite Valley, its diverse garden of trees, meadows, flowers, waterfalls, mountains and so on, take note of people with their sets of gifts, skills, talents and tools and write it down or record it. It might look something like this. "I saw Paul today; he was playing his guitar. Wow he is so talented! He played 'Perhaps Love.' His guitar sounds amazing. I love to watch his fingers dance so effortlessly across the fretboard while his beautiful voice rings out in concert with his hands. It moves me to tears. What an amazing use of gifts, skill, talents, and tools! Thank you so much Paul for using them!" Here is another example, "Today I watched with amazement as Jennifer facilitated the class. Her knowledge is so comprehensive. She ties the element together with real life stories which make the concepts come alive in my mind and it is so clear. All of her students watch her as we sit on the edge of our chairs. She is a master teacher." Here is another example from a slightly different perspective: "My friend Meg (not her real name) is having a difficult time. She is a cutter, one who needs to literally cut herself to the point of bleeding to get the pain out of her life for a moment. She has a beautiful way of writing about her life experience which is being developed and matured. When she writes I can feel her pain and I want to learn more. I wish she was more aware of her gift." Virtually everyone has a set of gifts, skills, talents and tools, such as they are. When you and I control our thoughts about people and when we become more aware of their gift set, even when those people are not aware of their own gifts, then our experience of life will be like a walk in Yosemite where the beauty of nature is differentiated in dramatic ways before our eyes. Have you ever seen the Dogwood dance in the spring breeze? Have you ever noticed how easily that girl works through those problems? It is so beautiful.

Before I leave the idea of controlling your thoughts when it comes to loving people and being more kind at home and work I want to take you through another thought exercise. You may have thought about this before. It is very profound and meaningful. I hope you will allow it to speak deeply to your soul. It is so important that you know how amazing people are… how amazing YOU are as a living human being. Let me begin with you first, then let this thought extrapolate to the way you think about every person, at home and in the world. Ready?

> *Consider the odds that you would be alive today. First, consider the odds that our lonely green planet could even exists in these unfathomable universes. The fact that we have not yet found thinking feeling life anywhere but here is truly incredible. What are the odds? What are the odds that human beings would come to existence here? It is truly amazing. Have you ever thought about how intricately your human body is made? How is it that your body takes oxygen from the air and distributes it to the far reaching extremes of your fingertips and toes, that your liver silently cleanse toxins, that neurons collaborate with each other so that I can communicate with you like this over space and time at the speed of light? What are the odds? What are the odds that your ancient ancestors would survive predators, disease, famines, natural disasters, genocides, wars and all the vicissitudes of life for long enough to be able to pass their DNA through the thousands of years to you? What are the odds? What are the odds that your mother and father would meet, come together and create your life? What are the odds that that one ovum and that one sperm, with their unique set of chromosomes would unite and become you? Are aware that your mother was born with millions of eggs? All of them passed into oblivion except you and your siblings. What are the odds. And of the countless sperm that your father created in his entire life, every single life giving sperm passed into nothingness, except for the one, yes only one of millions perhaps billions of perishing sperm cells experienced thinking feeling existence. What are the odds? The odds of you being*

alive today are so astronomical and beyond calculation (though some have made the attempt). The fact that you are alive is literally miraculous. Indeed, you are a freaking miracle of astronomical proportions. Some may be tempted to say, "Yes but there are billions and billions of people on the planet. What is so miraculous about that?" And, as I write this I shake my head in disbelief at those who are unable to see the miracle of billions of unique individuals differentiated by their gifts, skills, talents and tools, I would say to them, "Yes, billions of them! What a greater miracle is that!" The human being, yes all human beings, are the most amazing entities in the universe. And when you think of the other and yourself like this, that is, when you control your thoughts to think like this, it makes you want to bow with reverence and awe at each person. Any other way of thinking about the other and yourself, any negative, cavalier thought or action simply fails to align with the reality of the universe. It is a tragic failure. The universe compels us, it demands that we think of the other and ourselves as nothing less than miraculous to be thought of with respect, honor and reverence. Think this out loud with me, "I am, yes, we are, freaking amazing miracles of astronomical proportions."

Being kinder and more loving at home and work begins with controlling your thoughts about the other and yourself. The first thought we should have of each other is that we are freaking amazing miracles of astronomical proportions and we should always and in every way honor our self and the other! And when it is not the first thought we should correct our thought and remember the truth.

Now… if I were you I would be thinking about the way I treat the other and myself and I would be thinking,

> "That is a really cool way to think about people but that is not the way I normally think about people or myself. Honestly I see a lot, a whole lot of flaws in myself from the way I look to the way I feel about my life. Maybe I feel okay about myself but I wouldn't say I am amazing. And I am certain that my ex is nowhere near 'amazing.' My ex has dozens of issues! Even if they were 'amazing' I'm pretty sure someone dropped them on their heads at birth because some people are just lost causes, unredeemable, and destined to live as a somewhat worthless human being! And I'm not talking about just one or two!"

Call me Pollyanna, the eternal optimist, but I just cannot go there. I can't think about people as lost. I've been to the dark side and I have seen how bad some people can be. There is a reason for that and most of the time I just don't know why some people do what they do. Yet, I am not moved from what I see as mostly miraculous people. For me the overwhelming evidence is that people are good, creative, humanitarian, kind, want the best for children and the world, and are doing everything they can to survive. The idea of a "confirmation bias" is almost colloquial these days (search it if you haven't heard of confirmation bias), but the perspective that people are freaking amazing miracles of astronomical proportions is not wishful thinking. It is grounded in the history of family life and the survival of humanity. We haven't survived by accident. People truly care! Moreover, every new invention of technology, engineering, science, and medicine, points to the fact that people are amazing! If you have disbelief about your own amazing nature I would have to say that it just might be because of your conditioning in your environment or the prevailing culture and not in your nature as a human being. Your raw human being is beyond amazing and miraculous!

Our brains have been programed by family and culture since birth. Those neuro pathways are deep and wide! And, thankfully, you can escape both the programing of your negative family experience and cultural expectations… because you can control your thoughts. AND your brain is the most marvelous thing in the universe and it will work for you as you train it. You won't need to work 10,000 hours to master controlling your thoughts. In just a few minutes a day you can start building new eight lanes freeway-like neuropathways in your brain to carry electric impulses to places you never dreamed or imagined. You will have to learn to focus your attention and engage in System Two thinking, which is something you already know how to do, naturally. Here's the deal; ultimately you could even change your identity by controlling your thinking and becoming more loving. You could be "A Loving and Kind Person," differentiated by your loving gifts, skills, talents, and tools. When all is said and done love and kindness really are the most important things in the world. Being a loving kind person is the greatest thing that anyone could ever aspire to be.

Chapter 4
The Truth About Your Life

Next, I want to share my "Confirmation" *The Truth About My Life*. You, perhaps, have heard of "affirmations," right? Affirmations are popular in business productivity training programs. Real estate trainers will help you engage in a positive mindset by reciting affirmations like "I am a great salesperson!" or "People are naturally attracted to me." These are fun and help direct people to a future reality. A "Confirmation" on the other is the validation or confirmation of a present reality or truth. What follows is a confirmation I wrote for myself. It is not a projection to an aspired state of being. It is the current reality of my existence. I have it posted at my workstation and there are days when I need to control my thoughts so I read it aloud. This helps me. Please feel free to use it to control your thoughts. This is the truth about your life!

The Truth About My Life

The fact that I am alive today is an astounding amazing miracle of astronomical proportions. When I consider the odds of my existence in the Universe I am totally and completely amazed! My life, me, I am a miracle. Plus, I am endowed with and have acquired gifts, skills, talents and tools for my personal benefit and for the benefit of others. There is no doubt that I will use my gifts, skills, talents and tools today. This is love; when I use my gifts, skills, talents and tools for others. My love flows through others and has a ripple effect which extends beyond what I can see and know, even into future generations. My life and my love is meaningful and I make a difference. I will encounter problems because life is essentially a series of problems interspersed with periods of tranquility. I am competent and deal with problems well. When I encounter problems, even unexpected and life threatening problems, I solve them and become exponentially stronger in the process. I am antifragile. I control my thoughts so I replace negative thoughts because they are distractions which keep me from expressing my love. I just refocus my thoughts on what's most important. In fact, I welcome negativity and failure because they help me grow, become better, and achieve even exceed my goal. I gain from loss. As I think about my life I am deeply thankful, eternally grateful for this opportunity. I remember those who have come and gone before me and I honor them by living the best life possible, this is what they want for me. I realize that my life is a precious gift and there is no time to waste, even a moment. Yet I am not anxious, I am competent. I welcome the day. I welcome the challenge. I delight in the victory. My life is a miracle and love flows through me. Today my love will make a difference in the world. So be it!

Chapter 5
The Necessity of Doing Little Things from Your Loving Heart

Next to controlling your thoughts what you actually do for others and yourself is the most important aspect of love. When you listen to songs of the popular culture you will hear things like "I would die for you!" and "I would give you everything!" Which is good. Right? The real question that needs to be asked is "Will you take out the trash for me?" and "Will you rub my feet?" Real love is composed of thousands of little things that people do for each other never expecting anything in return. They just do it because they are loving people and they love doing little things for the other. You should underline those last two sentences because they are the very essence of love.

I must issue a warning. Do not do loving little things thinking that you will get some reward, or that you will get something back in return. I promise you that if you do you will be sorely disappointed and end up living a lonely life! I discovered this counselling troubled couples. Imagine that you are a fly on the wall overhearing my conversation with a man struggling to get his wife back.

> "I've tried everything to get her back! I bought her flowers. I took her out to a fine dinner. I told her how beautiful she is. Nothing seems to work!"

> Trying to control the stunned look on my face because he does get how wrong his statement is I say, "She sees all of those attempts as manipulations trying to get her to come back to you."

> And he says, "Well, I'm trying! Doesn't she see how much I want her back?"

> Sternly but compassionately I reply," This is not about YOU wanting her back. It is about HER BEING SAFE being in the relationship. Your attempts to get her back simple underscore that SHE IS NOT SAFE in the relationship because it is all about YOU getting what YOU want."

> Then he throws his hands up into the air and says "Well what the heck does she want?"

> And then I tell him the truth that he may not be able to hear, "She wants to be with a loving person who is genuinely loving all the time…not just when he wants something. Frankly you are 'acting' like a loving person but the reality is that you are simply trying to get something YOU want."

So the question I have for you, dear reader, is (and this is the question for every person, male, female, young and old.); Are you being a loving person or are you just acting like one for a purpose?"

The answer is YES! You are a loving person, and so are the other people in your life. You are designed to be a loving person. They and you may have forgotten how to love or have let other things take priority over love, but people are loving, born that way and for a loving purpose. Most people just need to be reminded about love and learn new ways to love more and deeper. My goal is to remind you about your loving self. Ultimately I want you to have as your primary identity "I am a loving person" and this being higher and more important to you than, "I am a good mom" or "I am a great father" or "I am great spouse" or "I am rich" or "I am a great leader" or "I am famous" or "I am successful" or "I am outstanding in my field." My dream for you is that the label you use to identify yourself as a person and the one you take the most pride in is "I am a Loving Person." I imagine you at a party meeting new people and someone says to you, "What do you do?" And you reply, "I am a loving person :-)." Nothing will distinguish you more as a loving person than doing little things from a loving heart. (Underline that sentence). The only reason or purpose a person would do loving little things is that little things naturally flow from a loving heart (You should underline that statement, too).

Before you move on to the three types of kindness I would like you to take a little quiz on the Kindness Mindset. Don't worry, you will do just fine! Just check the box next to each statement.

Kindness Mindset Quiz

1. There is a certain mindset that I can engage in and I can be more intentional about Kindness. [ ]
2. All my thoughts, feelings, and emotions are biological processes of my brain/body and I can control them. [ ]
3. I have two types of thoughts, System One automatic thoughts and System Two intentional thoughts. My loving kindness is an intentional System Two process. [ ]
4. There are two ways to think about people and myself. I control the way I think about people. People are freaking amazing miracles of astronomical proportions and so am I! [ ]
5. I am a loving person and my loving acts of kindness naturally flow from my loving heart, not the desire to gain anything. [ ]

Congratulations! You are on the road to mastering the Kindness Mindset. Way to go! I am proud of you! You are amazing. Now, let's learn about three types of kindness.

Part Two

Three Transformational Types of Kindness

There are three types of kindness; kind thoughts, kind words, and kind acts. Here are a few thoughts about kindness. Picture this; you are a parent driving your kids to school and you are late. As you are stalled in traffic the children are and have been constantly bickering, poking and provoking each other. Your irritation grows to the point that you cannot stand another moment and you scream at the top of your voice, "If you kids don't stop it and start being kind to each other I'm going to reach back and slap you both!" Which only makes them complain about the other, become defensive, and blame the other. To which you scream, "I said BE KIND damn it!" I've done that before and writing about it now make me laugh.

The word "kind" is an adjective, as in kind lady, and is associated with qualities like benevolence, compassion, being humane, empathetic, and considerate. The opposite of kind is callous, crude, contemptuous, uncaring, and inconsiderate.

My question is why would anyone be unkind? I know, it is a good question isn't it? The answer is… sometimes we just don't know. We can guess about what the unkind person is experiencing. But without a great deal of investigation we just don't know. The point is that there is something wrong with the unkind person and we recognize it.

I want to write a children's song about why some people are mean and not kind. It would go something like this. "Why, oh why did John make that girl cry? He said some awful things and I do not know why? Maybe he has a problem at home? I don't know. Maybe he feels out of control? I don't know. Maybe his underwear is crawling up his butt? I don't know. But surely something is wrong with John because he is not acting very kind. I hope he gets over it real soon, or someone will think he has been dropped on his head. Poor John."

What cause unkindness in families is often just plain old frustration. Most people were born into and raised in families where bonding, emotional connecting, and love reigned. Yes, families have difficulty and hardship. Most families welcomed their babies with deep love and a genuine desire to nurture and do the very best for that child. Nevertheless, as Jennifer Senior has noted in her book "All Joy and No Fun: The Paradox of Modern Parenting," parenting can be very taxing. This is especially true in parenting teenagers. Teenagers can be very persistent and they have developed good reasoning and communication skills. Many parents have experienced episodes of conflict when a demanding teen insists on prevailing in a request even after several denials from the parent. I have heard teens say to their parents, "You are being unreasonable!" This can be very, very frustrating. Here is a kind response in a very frustrating confrontation with a teen: "I have heard your request and your reasoning and I am denying your request simply because I am the parent and you are the child. I am sorry you don't understand. This is my final decision." There is nothing unkind about firm resolve with not yet fully developed teens. Kindness at home can be very challenging. Later I will introduce you to The Kindness Culture Statement which you can use to help create a kindness culture at home.

I have found kindness in every city I have been in even in Washington D.C. I know you might not believe it. But I assure you while politics seems to have drowned out the voice of kindness, kindness is written in the DNA of human beings. Kindness is found in every nation, even when there is international tension. I am sure that nations would rather be kind than otherwise. The truth is kindness is the desired and preferred state. The truth also is that everyone, parents, children, business people, politicians, heads of states, religions leaders, everyone would gain from learning more about how to be kind. The truth is kindness is more of a System Two process and requires intentional action from a loving heart. Here are some ways to think about and grow in kindness.

Chapter 6
Kind Thoughts

The first type of kindness is kind thoughts. "I only think good things about Jennifer all the time, except when I don't, and then I change it." That's a funny little sentence that I tell myself and others. I didn't always think that way about Jennifer. Jennifer and I were very young when we married. I tell people I was 10 and she was 12. That is not true, of course, but it is a fun thing to say and underscores that fact that we married young. When you consider that the human brain does not fully mature until the mid-twenties (or later) you might say that we, especially me, were not fully mature in our thinking when we married. I think it is kinder to say "not fully mature in our thinking" than saying "someone dropped him on his head at birth." I thought there was something wrong with Jennifer's thinking process and I would correct her frequently. We had many arguments about the correct way to proceed in many areas of life, like whether or not vinegar belongs in the refrigerator, the toilet paper should be dispensed from the top, you know, important things like that.

It was more serious when I needed to correct her about money issues, family situations, dealing with health problems and ways of being in society and culture. Jennifer is a very smart woman with a razor sharp memory and consequently we often had animated disagreements (You know what "animated disagreements" are don't you?). Then one day I came to my senses. Maybe I had an epiphany or maybe my brain finally fully developed and I realized that Jennifer was a competent human being able to negotiate her way through the world … without my assistance! I also realized I was not responsible for her thoughts and actions and I, as her husband, did not need to rule her life (It is somewhat embarrassing to write how I use to think). She may have been a child bride, but she was not MY child. Frankly, my thinking about her then had more to do with what I thought people might think about me if she thought, spoke or acted in a way that I was uncomfortable with. Yes, I was like the man in counselling above; it was all about me. I was mostly unaware of what I thought and operated primarily from System One. That is corrected now (mostly). It only took me 20 years, one marital crisis and several marriage and family counselling sessions. I only think good things about her always, and when I don't I correct it and return to thinking good things. In the process I discovered that she truly is a freaking amazing human being. She is an extremely competent parent, businesswoman, financial manager, planner, creator, negotiator and partner in life. She has the most amazing set of acquired and innate gifts, skills, talents, and tools! Still sometimes it is challenging to listen to her conversations. She still says and does things differently than I would, and I have to control myself as I watch her genius unfold. I recognize that my uncomfortableness is mine to own and has nothing to do with her. She never ceases to amaze me. "I only have good thoughts about her." Isn't that nice?

You might think that this is a great gift to her, that I only think good things about her. I am sure that our relationship is massively better. I see it is a great gift to me, also. Instead of being on edge about what she might say or do in every situation I watch her as the student would watch a great master create a piece of art. It is thrilling to watch as the block of granite is being transformed into a beautiful sculpture before my eyes. I love that experience and I learn so much in the process. Thinking about Jennifer this way has made my life so much better. Now, here is the greater thing. Are you ready? This is the way I think about everyone! People are amazing!

When I engage you in a conversation you might notice that behind my eyes, which are totally devoted to you at the moment, I am thinking to myself, "Before me stands an amazing miracle of astronomical proportion endowed with and having developed gifts, skills, talents, and tools which she uses for her benefit and the benefit of others. I must dignify and honor this moment." Yes, I know that this is a process which requires intention. That is the System Two part of the process. Sometimes this is not my first response. My first response may be "How is it that this person does not see that I am focusing my attention on the task at hand and that her inquiry is a disruptive intrusion." Sometimes that thought is expressed in more colorful language in my mind. That is when I stop it. I slip into System Two and think only good thoughts. You will remember, we can control our thoughts, even I can. Thinking this way about people makes the human experience much more interesting!

May I tell you a story about how thinking good thoughts in an unexpected situation. I think you will like it. I was in Lincoln Nebraska with my son's family visiting the University of Nebraska as a possible place for my grandsons to go to college. The day before we walked a lot and my foot, still tender from an accident, recommended that I not walk so much. While they went back to the University for more touring I found a nice shady bench in the busy area near a farmer's market close to our hotel. I had started reading my own book, "My Ideal Day of Love: 24 Hours of Love at Home and Work," on our flight to Lincoln and I was wanting to finish it (By the way, it is such a good book!). Near the bench a street musician was playing his guitar. I have an affinity for street musicians because they are artists using their gifts, skills, talents, and tool for their benefit and the benefit of others. They perform a good service for the community. I listened and read. Nearby there was a young homeless man lying on the sidewalk supporting his back by leaning against the street light pole. He was a mess. He couldn't have been more than in his mid-thirties but his missing teeth and gaunt face made him look more like my age except his hair was full of youthful natural red color. My first thought was wondering if he was planning on stealing the guitarist lone dollar in the guitar case. Now where I was sitting the guitarist could not see me and was unaware of my presence. The two of us, the homeless man and I were the only ones paying attention to the guitarist. After one song, the guitarist looked over to the homeless man and said, "How you doin, Man?" The homeless man shrugged his head as if to say, "You know how it is."

Then the guitar man played another tune. It was a song about the hardships of life and it had a very catchy refrain. After the second verse when it was time for the refrain the homeless man sang the refrain with the guitar man with a huge smile on his face! I was amazed because he was singing along to a song that he obviously had never heard before. It was that catchy of a tune. During the third verse the homeless man nodded his head approvingly to the beat and sang the refrain again with gusto after the verse. When the song ended, the homeless man got up, said, "That was great man!" threw a few coins in the guitar case and walked away down the street toward the vendors with a big smile on his face. The guitar man continued to sing another song and said, "Thanks, Man." After that song I approached the guitar man. "Did you see that guy singing and nodding to that tune?" He replied, "Yeah I wrote that song and I thought he would like it." I said, "You got him singing and nodding and you transformed him. That was amazing! Thank you so much for sharing your gift." He said, "That is why I sing, so that it might help somebody, why else?" he said pointing to the lone dollar and few coins in the guitar case. "I thought he might like it." This was a labor of love. I said, "Thank you so much, that was amazing to watch. You have a wonderful gift."

The way I thought about the homeless man is the way that many people might think about homeless people, threatened by them and afraid of what they might do. The way the street musician thought about the homeless man was with empathy and compassion and he demonstrated it by singing a song he thought the homeless many could identify with and enjoy. To be clear, the kindness in this story was the kind thought the street musician had about the homeless man.

When we have kind thoughts about the other transformation can happen. Remember, "I always think good thoughts about you 100% of the time, except when I don't, then I stop and think good thoughts about you again." People are amazing!

Chapter 7

Kind Words

The second type of kindness is kind words. I am fascinated by words and their power. Some people use the "f" word to emphasis a point, or for its shock power, or because they identify with a particular sub-cultural. It is just a word and its impact is experienced broadly. When I listen to serial entrepreneur and social media guru Gary Vaynerchuk at home I must use my earpods so my elderly Mother-in-law won't be exposed to his prolific use of the "f" word. It offends her greatly. Vaynerchuk's audiences seem to enjoy the passion and enthusiasm associated with the word's use.

Words are powerful and can destroy people. It is difficult for me to write about words that destroy. I feel compelled to write about it so that we can do some self-reflection about the way we talk with others, especially our loved ones. It just BLOWS MY MIND that people who are in supposedly loving relationships will say such mean, contemptuous, nasty and ugly words to each other, even children! I will not give an example here because they are so powerful that they linger in the mind a long time and will distract you from the task of reading about kindness. When mean contemptuous words are used it is like a sharp wide-blade knife violently thrust into a person's soul being twisted and stabbed again and again creating grievous emotional damage and unbearable enduring pain. (Underline that last sentence.) The childhood saying is wrong, words can hurt even kill the spirit. When mean contemptuous words are used it is a sure sign that there is something deeply wrong with the user. (Underline that sentence, too.) I don't know exactly what is wrong. I know that there is something terribly wrong with the user of hurtful and contemptuous words. I only ask that you search your life for hurtful words. They are like a nuclear bomb with their devastation. Please vow to never, never use hurtful and contemptuous words in your life time. Remove 100% of unkind words from your vocabulary.

If words have the power to destroy words have an even greater power to build up. Words can even create life from nothing according to ancient traditions. Words build up, encourage, and motivate others. Kind words restore the damaged human soul. Here a couple of ways we use kind words at home and work.

Jennifer and my real estate brokerage work culture allows for occasional opportunities to "fill someone's bucket" with affirming words. At a recent business meeting attendees were asked to use a single word to describe a co-worker. Each one rose from their seats, directed their attention to the co-worker and spoke a single affirming word describing her like, caring, knowledgeable, wise, accountable, encouraging, supportive and badass (in this setting this is a kind word).

These affirming words spoken from the heart had a very meaningful impact on the recipient.

My family has a birthday ritual which has been passed down through the generations and overflows into our business and friends. At birthday gatherings, at work and home, we tell the birthday person why we love them. Beginning with the youngest person at the event, one by one we state one thing we love about them. This is a wonderful use of words. It is very affirming and heartwarming. We often see tears of joy and appreciation from the speaker and the recipient.

Kind words spoken to someone experiencing a difficult time can literally save the other's life by igniting a spark of hope in a deep dark time of life. Kind words raise the defeated from their ashes and restore the depleted.

Here are some of the most important kind words ever spoken. The most frequently used kind word is "Thank you." The spirit of gratitude generated by Thank You is universally felt and experienced. It cannot be overused. Let me tell you why. Thank You speaks of the necessity of community, our interdependence and our shared existence. It is an honoring of the other and our acknowledgement of an act of contribution to the well-being of the community. "Thank you" could be for opening the door, taking out the trash, discovering previously unknown aspects of medicine, science or particle physics. When we say "Thank you" we say "Your act of honoring me is received with sincere gratitude" or "What you did is important for the well-being of our community and we acknowledge you and your contribution." The awarding of the Nobel prize is a ritual of "Thank you" as is the kind response to taking out the trash.

"I love you" must be some of the most important words in the universe. It is so precious that former generations reserved it for important occasions. Once I complained to my Dad that I could not remember a time when he said "I love you" to me. He paused and said, "Look at how I have cared for you and nurtured you from your birth until today. I provided for you, I took care of your every need and why? My actions show you 1000 time more how I think about you. Is not my love for you perfectly clear by my actions?" What he said was true, of course. To this day I am not sure if my desire and need to hear "I love you" is rooted in the conditioning of the prevailing culture, or if it is a genuine human need to hear the words. What I do know is that the words "I love you" are very meaningful. I am aware that the words "I love you" must be backed up by actions demonstrating the reality of the fact. Yes, "I love you" is frequently said cavalierly, recklessly, and without any forethought and is used as a System One response. Historically it was more of a System Two action. Nevertheless "I love you" is in fact very impactful and when said with intention has a profound effect on the other. When I say "I love you" and you discern from my face, voice tone, body language and actions, that it is genuine, authentic, and from the heart you unconsciously recognize that I am safe, that my intention for you is life-giving and affirming. Not only do I accept you as you are but I feel an emotional bond, a connection and oneness with you. You can relax, be vulnerable, trusting and you can reciprocate. You can let your guard down in the presence of love. You are affirmed, not just as another human being, but in your personhood and your very special individual identity. "I love you" says that among all the people on earth you are special to me, I desire you, the person, ontologically, that is, from the center of my being. We can be intimate at a profound level. Practice saying "I love you" with those you love.

Other powerful kinds words are compliments, congratulations and appreciation. Ellen Langer, pioneer of mindfulness and author of the book Mindfulness, states that the essence of mindfulness is noticing the difference. I have learned to pay attention and I notice when someone wears a new outfit, got a haircut, or lost or gained a few pounds (I don't mention a weight gain, unless it is a good weight gain.) and I say something kind like, "That is a nice hair cut" or "You look pretty in pink." Nonagenarian Margie walks into church pushing her walker. She often wears pink. When I see her I say, "Margie, you are pretty in pink." She giggles and smiles. Those kind compliments make people feel good. Have you ever wondered why people like and need compliments? I noticed that sometimes after I have given an especially good talk I want to fish around for a compliment. Sometimes I can resist the urge to say "What did you think about my talk?" I tell myself, "That the talk was good, technically good, great style, good audience response, delivered with energy and persuasive, and the audience was engaged, nodding with agreement, laughing at the humor, and clapped at the end. I really don't need anyone to tell me it was great. It was in fact a great talk. I don't need anyone's compliment." So I find it interesting that I still want the compliment. If I, the professional speaker, need, want or desire affirmation, how much more the occasional speaker? It is easy to apply this example to many other areas. People want and need affirmation. It validates their gifts, skills, talents and tools, their differentiated role in that particular community and spurs them on. Affirmations validate their identity. It confirms that they are on track with their gifts, skills, talents and tools. Compliments, congratulations and appreciations are very powerful and speak deeply to people. As a member of that particular community, group, team, or cohort it is actually our duty to support, encourage, and empower the individual members to function at their best for the benefit of all the members. A kind word is an essential element for community and individual health.

What is not helpful and should be removed from human interaction is so called "constructive criticism." Constructive criticism is an oxymoron. The misuse of constructive criticism is widespread. More people are hurt than helped by it. It is an old and outdated technology and morally wrong. Offering constructive criticism is like using tin cans and a string to communicate. There are far better ways to communicate and far better ways to change behavior. I use pedagogic questions to guide my students to self-discovery and improvement. I never offer constructive criticism and I hope that after reading this you will stop too.

Which brings me to this final thought about Kind Words; control your words! Remove every unkind word from your vocabulary. Stop using unkind words, period. Make your goal to only speak kind words 100% of the time. Have a zero tolerance for unkind words in your vocabulary. You know the destructive power of unkind words and the incredible power of kind words so vow to never use unkind words. This will be a process and you will need to remind yourself often to only use kind words. You will need to use

System Two thinking to analyze why you slip and use unkind words. When you analyze your slips you will discover that the other person did not make you say unkind words. You said something unkind because something triggered your anger, fear, disgust or powerlessness in a situation and the unkind words were your immediate System One response. When this happens there are two things you must do. First, be kind to yourself. Your instant response is a deeply rooted human response to protect yourself. Your self-protection is necessary for survival and is of utmost importance. Your slip was merely not under the control of your neocortex at that particular moment. It was a primitive response. So be kind to yourself and regain control of your thought. Second, simply return to using kind words. Switch back. No harm, no foul. If you did create damage with unkind words you can repair the damage by explaining that you had a bad moment (a brain fart, if you will) temporarily lost some control, apologize and move forward with kindness. I'm an expert at that! In summary, make it your goal to only use kind, life giving, affirming words 100% of the time and remove every negative word, 100%, from your life. It is written, "Kind words are like honey sweet to the soul and healthy for the body."

Chapter 8

Kind Acts

Nothing demonstrates real love more than kind acts. Kind acts are the full revelation of love. Your kind acts are the combination of kind thought and kind words. When I think about kind acts the picture that comes to my mind is that of Pope Francis kissing the troubled boy during his 2015 American tour. I wrote about this in my book "My Ideal Day of Love" in a chapter called "Touch." Touch is a little thing and a kind act. Here is what I wrote.

> *During Pope Francis' historic 2015 visit to the United States of America there was a moving moment when the Pope stopped his car, got out, reached out to a boy with cerebral palsy, touched him and kissed him. The news report noted that the boy's father was so moved by the event that he had to turn away. Francis' touch conveyed love, compassion, healing, hope, and recognition. The family will forever tell the story of the Pope's love and touch.*
>
> *The power of touch has been well documented. It is a stress reliever, lowers heart rate, blood pressure and cortisol*

levels and stimulates positive hormones and neurochemicals. The psychological and spiritual effects of touch are profound, as mentioned earlier. In addition, touch is empowering.

What proceeds touch as an empowering agent is dysphoria and its debilitating effects of helplessness in its various forms. This has been seen in infants and young children who fail to thrive. Without touch they languish between being and not being to the point of death. But when held, touched and caressed they make gains. It is so natural for capable parents to hold, snuggle, and touch their babies that we think nothing of it. It is just what we do. What we don't know is how essential that touch is for the child's well-being. We fail to realize that without touch the baby won't develop normally. We touch mindlessly, automatically, unconsciously. It is like breathing or hearts beating; essential for life, but not a conscious effort. Touch is essential for human development and touch is an automatic natural response.

So, while it seems amazing that Pope Francis would touch a maladjusted child it is merely a human reaction to restore or empower another. It is just love. And while you and I are not the Pope we contain in us the same power to heal, restore and empower. We can do it naturally, unconsciously, automatically in response to the dysphoric one. Think about it… it is what you mindlessly do. In the presence of a trauma, major or minor, you hurry to attend the victim and you reach out and touch them, "Are you alright?" And here is the epiphany; we can touch, heal and empower mindfully!

Pope Francis saw the need while he was slowly driving by. He stopped the car. He walked directly to the boy. He mindfully and intentionally reached out and touched the

boy. You and I can do the same. Stay alert! Be mindful of the
people around you. You will discover dozens of opportunities
to deliver healing, empowering touch.

This story is a good case study on kind acts and how they work. To begin let's look at it from the perspective of the giver of the kind act. I think you will agree with me that you do not have to be the Pope to give kind acts so let's humanize him and simply call him Francis, the human being. As a human being Francis is endowed with and has developed specific gifts, skills, talents and tools which differentiates him from others and he uses them for his benefit and for the benefit of others. We are going to assume that Francis is not going to perform this kind act for his own benefit. He might feel good after performing the kind act but that would be more about confirming his role in maintaining well-being of the community, the satisfaction of being a contributing member rather than any adulation or praise he might receive. We are also going to assume that Francis knows that when he exercises his gift it will have a positive effect. His life experience bears this out. Let's also assume that Francis, as a loving kind person, is mindful, or aware of his surroundings and looks for opportunities to be loving, perform acts of kindness, and use his gift. So this leads us to Francis noticing the boy. He stops everything, the car, the guards, and focuses on the boy. In a moment he realizes there is an opportunity to use his gift.

Think about this with me. What is his opportunity? Is it just to perform a kind act? I think not. Francis is aware that in addition to performing a kind act here is an opportunity to model the kind of behavior he would like others to engage in. This is a kind moment plus it is a teaching moment. In other words, the effect of his kindness is greater than the act itself. It has a multilayered and ripple effect. Please note that. It is important also to note that once he see the opportunity he is very intentional and purposeful in the act. That is, while this seems to be a random act it is, in reality, a well thought out and deliberate act for which Francis is always ready and knowledgeable about effects of the act.

As Francis approaches the boy he is aware that he is being noticed and watched. This further deepens his awareness of the significance of the act. As he arrives at the boy he actually engages in several little things, several kind acts. First he smiles and greets all. This is extremely important as it signals his good intention to the people. A smile is probably the most common and important kind act of all. Next with fluid motion Francis reaches down, touches the boy, almost holding his head in his hands and then kisses him. This reveals two other kind acts which, as noted in the story, have profound effect, touch and a kiss.

Here Francis made a giant calculation, that the touch and kiss would be welcomed. An extreme amount of caution must be taken about touch and kiss. It would be a rare event, extremely rare, where I would give a touch or kiss that was not wanted. In fact, I nearly always ask permission to touch. I want all my touching to be wanted because I just do not know what the touch may mean to the other person. An unwanted touch could be damaging. In our case study here it must be assumed that the culture dictated that this touch and kiss was acceptable. My advice is to always ask to touch, do not assume it is okay.

Francis knows about the powerful effect of touch. A loving kind wanted touch conveys much more information than just compassion and warmth. Touch stimulates powerful chemicals in both the one being touched and the one giving the kind act. There is a moment when individuals become one and share their humanity. In that moment the isolation of self gives way to our community of love and support, restores hope and gives comfort. Francis knows this and he lingers a moment or two to allow the touch to fully manifest its work. Next Francis turns to the others and allows the ripple effect of his act to move into the hearts and lives of the other.

Finally, realizing the act of kindness has been effectively delivered, he returns to his car and continues on the way. The boy, his family and those around him have been blessed and world has been taught how the power of a kind act can affect the world.

It is important that you internalize this case study and learn from it. Please pay attention to what I am about to say, underline it: What Francis did is merely a human act, it is not just the act of a Pope. It is entirely a human act, an act that can be performed by anyone...even you!

Before we leave the story of Francis let's look at the event from the eyes of the boy and his family. My understanding is that the boy and his family are at that particular place and time because a relative is the music director and in a position to give his family a close up view of the Pope. Obviously they are a religious family and seeing the Pope would be a story they could tell for the rest of their lives. They excitedly watch the Pope drive by. Then, to their wonder, the car stops and the Pope got out. They think, "What is he doing?" Then they catch the Pope looking at them. Their hearts start racing as the Pope makes his way directly to them. His smile doesn't calm their beating hearts, yet they feel the warmth of it. The rush of excitement makes the whole experience seem surreal. Their autonomic response reveals their bodies chemical reaction to the event (Which, by the way, Francis can observe.). The experience is beginning to be permanently embedded in their memories. What happens next is a whirlwind. The Pope touches the boy, holds his head and kisses him. It is all over in a moment as the Pope greets and touches family, friends, and then, as quickly as he came he drives off. They turn to each other, "What just happened? Did you see that? The Pope, His Holiness, just kissed the boy and he touched me too!" This is the story they will forever tell; the day the Pope changed their lives.

Here are some key ideas that the kind act of Francis reveals.

1. Kind acts may seem to be random but the giver is always looking for an opportunity to give a kind act. It is a mindful and an intentional response.

2. Kind acts are for the benefit of the other and there is a bounce back effect to the giver, a good feeling knowing one is using their gifts, skills, talents, and tools for the benefit of other.

3. Kind acts reverberate and have a ripple effect. The act is felt by those in near proximity and those who hear the story later, even years later.

4. Kind acts stimulate positive chemicals in the recipient and the giver. These chemicals promote well-being, physically, emotionally and spiritually.

5. The kind act of wanted touch conveys more information than meets the eye like, compassion, community, togetherness, oneness, empowerment, hope and love.

6. The foreknowledge that the act is going to be successful should embolden the giver to act. Act confidently and act more often.

7. Kind acts are human acts and not the domain of a few "special" people. Everyone is entitled to use kind acts. In fact, it is a human responsible to exercise kind acts.

The list of kind acts is limited only by the imagination. Wanted touch, as we have noted, is powerful and includes acts like hand holding, foot rubbing, massage, brushing hair, bathing, wrestling, hugs, sitting close to each other. This brings back the memory of a distant difficult time in Jennifer and my relationship. We had grown apart as I was so devoted to my work that it created emotional distance between us. We sought couple therapy. One intervention the therapist made was for Jennifer to sit on my lap for five minutes daily. That was a long time ago and that touch had a great benefit for us. Obviously, we still remember it. Here are more kind acts.

Giving Gifts

Giving gifts of flowers, candy, clothes, jewelry and money are all well-known kind acts. Once, when we were poor college students, Jennifer's high school friend brought bags of groceries and we were able to share with other poor college families. We have never forgotten her kind act and we have done the same for many others.

Distant Connections

Another category of kind acts is what I call "distant connections." These are acts like leaving a love note in your child's lunch box or backpack, your spouse's briefcase or purse, in their suitcase when they travel, a note in the underwear drawer, an unexpected carrier delivered special gift or a card snail mailed for no special occasion, not to mention love texts, emails, and direct messages. I'm sure you can be even more creative with your distant connections.

Paying Close Attention and Responding Positively

A phenomenal kind act is "paying close attention responding positively." I think it was at a John Gottman Couples Retreat where Jennifer and I learned about "bids" for attention. Bids for attention are messages we send to the other to get their attention. I particularly like it when Jennifer raises her eyebrows and motions her head for me to follow her. I will usually respond positively to that bid for attention. We observed bids for attention one day while sitting in the cafeteria at what was at that time called Yosemite Lodge in Yosemite National park. Watching people might seem creepy but we play a Sherlock Holmes like game trying to figure out where people come from and what they are talking about. Sometimes we compete in making up completely fantastic stories inspired by the people we watch. On this occasion we noticed one couple sitting there almost silent. He was reading the Fresno Bee and held the newspaper up so that it completely blocked his view of her and her view of him. I do not mean to disrespect the Fresno Bee but the last thing in the world that I would want to read in the beauty of that most fabulous setting, with the grand Yosemite Falls in the background, is the Fresno Bee. There he was completely engrossed in it. She was playing with her bowl of oatmeal and would lookup occasionally longingly hoping for some attention (that is a bid for attention). One time she gently tapped the bowl attempting to get his attention (that is a bid), next she quietly, but noticeably to us a table away, cleared her throat with an "Ahem" (that is another bid). Then she sighed deeply (another bid). It was so obvious, so sad and so funny. I was waiting for her to reach up and rip the newspaper out of his hands. One of the kindest things you can do for the other is to pay attention to them and respond to them positively. This means being mindful of them, their subtle clues, nonverbal requests, stop whatever activity you are doing, and being present for them. That is very kind indeed. It says, "I'm paying attention to you," "I like attending to you," "You are important to me."

Extraordinary Courtesies

Extraordinary Courtesies are simple kind acts such as opening the door for someone, standing when one enters the room, going shopping with the other, helping with tasks, like sharing in meal preparation and the cleanup, making the bed, taking out the garbage without being asked, folding laundry, assisting with clothing choices ("That one looks great on you!), having a beverage ready when they come home, and so on.

Smiles

Smiles, lots of smiles, are in a class of kindness all by themselves. My Jennifer is the Queen of Smiles. Me? Not so much. I have to work at smiling. I have post-it notes posted at my workstation saying "Smile" and "Smile More!" I think a smile is the supreme kind act. There is much to be said about smiling. It is very difficult to resist a smile and not smile back. Try it, even on the New York subway. I've done this. It is the unwritten rule that people don't smile or engage other people on the subway. It is sort of like men don't talk to each other in the restroom. Women do but men don't. You're not supposed to smile on the subway. So I did. I smiled and caught someone's eye. They immediately smiled and when they realized they had broken the rule of no smiling on the subway they immediately turned their head and looked down at the ground where no humans smile. They may have been thinking about how rude and troubled I must be. Jennifer's smile is amazing. When she smiles it is impossible not to return the smile. Her warmth springs up from deep within her, like Old Faithful, splashing up through her eyes, her forehead, her cheeks and, of course her lips, her whole face explodes with a smile. It is the most wonderful experience to receive her smile. It is so powerful, warm, beautiful and transforming. Beholding her smile releases endorphins, dopamine, and oxytocin, I am sure. My brain bathed in those smile induced chemicals experiences safety, trust, appreciation, respect, welcoming, sometimes with humor and laughing. Did you know the smile was so powerful? Don't you want to smile more and be smiled at? Of course you do.

Think about how much you could help with your smile. The smile is such a little thing and perhaps the greatest kind act.

Friendship

By its very nature friendship is kindness based. When you and I become friends it is a special type of relationship. We like each other, care about each other, want to spend time with each other, we play, work, eat and spend time together. We look out for each other, protect each other and we encourage each other. What can be more kind than being friends? There are a variety of friendship from best friends to friends we only see once every few years or decades. We have friends at work. Work friendship are very important because we spend so much time together. I heard one co-worker say her co-worker was her "work wife" implying a special kind of friendship. Some friendships last a lifetime. My elderly mother is still in contact with a childhood friend! Some friendships are very brief, like camp friends or friends made at conferences. Some friendships don't turn out so well.

The painful side of friendships is betrayal and abandonment. Unfortunately losing a friend is all too often one of the consequences of friendships. My philosophy is to make friends often and keep them as long as possible. Even after a friendship ends remember the good times, forgive the bad times, and keep former friends in your database. You may want to touch base with them in the future, even after a betrayal. Things change, you know.

I know this may sound crazy but make sure your spouse and your children are your friends. I know some couples who just kind of put up with each other for one reason or another. If you ask them if they were friends they respond, "Well, were married, so I guess we are friends?" Hum, that questioning tone says a lot, doesn't it? One of the kindest things you can do for your spouse is to be their friend (Jennifer is my best friend :-)). The same holds true for your children. It is very important that you remember that your role is to parent your developing children and you can be their friend too. Even Tiger Moms can be friends. And when your children are adults befriend them. Adult children will always view their aging parents as special and they can have fun with them also. Once, in my role as a real estate broker, I got a call requesting to show a house for sale. When I arrived at the house I met a woman in her 50s and her elderly 80+ year old mother. They were out looking at investment properties together. The home that I showed them just happened to be the childhood home of the elderly mother! It was a very strange coincident. They loved walking through the house and remembering. As we spent more time together it became apparent to me that the elderly mother had some dementia. Her daughter never mentioned the mother's dementia to me she just encouraged her mom along was pleasant and enjoyed being her friend looking for investment property. I loved that experience.

Please take a few moments now and think about your friends. I recommend that you do something kind for them like write a note of appreciation for their friendship. That would indeed be a kind thing to do. Friendship is a special kind of kindness.

Kindness Boot Camp for Kids

Let's talk about teaching children kindness. When I started to write this book I did not have it in my mind to write about Kindness Boot Camps for kids. Then one of the special people in my life was bullied at school. It created a significant reaction at home and school. It made me realize that we have a lot of kindness work to do at home, the office and school. So Jennifer and I are in the very beginning phases of starting our Kindness Boot Camps for Kids. We have had some very encouraging response. I found many kindness programs for kids and schools on-line. As I review this book I found it to be a great outline for a Kindness Boot Camp. This has encouraged us to move forward. Look for more about our Kindness Boot Camps. They are still just a glimmer in our eyes as I write this.

I think you will agree with me that children need to learn more about kindness for many reasons. There are three key places where children learn kindness; home, school, and social media/TV. My recommendation is that parents help children build a social media kindness presence using blogs, vlogs, or any social media platform to convey kindness information. Children could conduct kindness interviews, perform kindness skits, drama, comedies, music, puppets, song, dance, etc. to present the key elements in this book. Isn't that a great idea? By the way, this is exactly what Mr. Rogers did with the technology he had at that time. The reason it is important that parents get involved is that kindness really needs to be modeled at home. By helping children with a social media project you are killing two birds with one stone (Oh my! That doesn't sound kind! But you know what I mean). And you may want to include your children's classmates in the process. That way you can have a kindness impact at school. You won't need to make this a years long project. Plan out a series that runs for a few weeks and present it. You will have done a great job conveying and internalizing the information, skills and techniques that will last your children a lifetime even generations! I remember when our kids were elementary school age Jennifer and I started an afternoon Kids Club in our neighbor. Gosh! That is a great memory. Our kids still talk about it. Our daughter ran into an old neighborhood friend recently who said, "Do you remember the Kids Clubs your parents did?" That was many years ago and they now have children of their own. Your kindness program will change negative family and school habits into kindness habits and rituals. I honestly believe that you and I are the ones responsible for making the world kinder. These ideas are very achievable, would be a lot of fun, and make a kind impact at home, school, community, culture, and the world.

Chapter 9
My Kindness Culture Statement

"That's all I have to say about that." Forrest Gump is a kind fictional character. His IQ may not have been the highest but his kindness was off the charts. This may be a small book with little things ideas but it is off the charts with kindness. Here are some things that I hope you will remember.

> Probably the greatest thing you can do with your life is to *practice loving kindness*. Your kindness will make a huge difference with your family, friends and in the world. You will never regret being kind.

> You can *control your thinking*, your emotions and feelings, and your actions to a far greater degree than you ever thought or imagined possible. All of your thoughts, feelings and emotions are biological processes and you can control them!

> System One thinking naturally flows right out of you, for the better and the worse. *Loving kindness is a System Two process* and requires more time and effort.

Become more aware of your thinking and use System Two!

➤ 99% of all *human beings are freaking amazing miracles* of astronomical proportions… even you. Give every human being the respect and honor they deserve, even yourself!

➤ 1% evilness on the earth is a huge army. Keep yourself safe from them. *Self-protection is your built in survival system.* Your ancestors were so good at protecting their selves that their DNA has been passed down over thousands of years to you. *Keep yourself safe* too!

➤ There are three types of transformational kindnesses; kind thoughts, kind word and kind acts. *Kindness can save and transform lives!*

➤ Only *think kind thoughts about people and yourself 100% of the time*. And when you don't, stop yourself, control your thoughts and return to thinking kind thoughts again. You can do this!

➤ Words are more powerful than just about any force on earth. Eliminate every unkind word from your vocabulary. *Only use kind words all the time!*

➤ *You are capable and empowered to perform kind acts.* Always be looking for and ready to perform a kind act knowing that the results of your action will reverberate through people and time.

➤ Start a Kindness Boot Camp and *teach the material in this book.*

➤ *Your kind acts are the greatest manifestation of your love.*

- *Ascribe to, fully embrace, teach at home and post the "My Kindness Culture Statement"* which follows next. Please feel free to adapt it to suit your home and business.

- Be on the lookout for my next book "Eternity is the E in L.O.V.E.: Experiencing Meaning and Changing the World." There are four books in this series.

I want you to know that as I have been writing these words I have been thinking about you. I imagine you in your particular setting and I think about what must be happening in your life. I think good thoughts about you all the time. My earnest hope, dream and desire for you is that the collective loving kindness of the entire universe flows through your heart and mind to your world. I love you!

My Kindness Culture Statement

- ❖ *Kindness begins by controlling my thoughts, feelings, and emotions. My thoughts, feelings and emotions are biological processes of my brain and body and there are many ways I can control them, like simply thinking about something else or focusing my attention on something better.*

- ❖ *Kindness is a System Two process, not always easy, often requiring work and effort. I am aware of when I am using automatic System One processes and when I need to use System Two.*

❖ *I control the way I think about people. People are amazing, in fact, people, like me, are miraculous! So I will dignify, honor and respect people and myself.*

❖ *There are three types of kindness; kind thoughts, kind words and kind acts. I will be aware of every opportunity to be kind.*

❖ *I always think kind thoughts about people and when I don't I will stop, engage System Two, control my thoughts and think good things again. I believe that almost all human beings are great people with their own set of gifts, skills, talents and tools. Even when I strongly disagree with people I respect them and I am kind.*

❖ *I only use kind words. I completely eliminate negative words from my vocabulary. When I use unkind words it is a sign that there is something going on inside me that needs to be attended to and I figure out how to fix it. I especially use "Thank you" and I tell my loved ones "I love you."*

❖ *My kind acts are important and effective. They ripple through time even into future generations. I am always looking for opportunities to do kind acts especially smiles, wanted touch, gifts, distant connections, paying close attention and responding positively, extraordinary courtesies, friendship, and thousands of different kinds of little things, like rubbing feet and taking out the trash.*

❖ *I search for opportunities to organize kindness initiatives like Kindness Boot Camps to teach others about kindness, especially children.*

❖ *I am a kind loving person. Loving kindness flow through my mind and my heart to my world. I make a difference with my love and kindness.*

❖ *My home is known as a kind place where all members practice kindness 100% of the time! And when something unkind happens we figure out what the problem is, fix it and return to our normal natural state of kindness.*

About Bryan Lee Martin

I am a loving person. I am married to Jennifer. We raised four children and a few others. We have eleven grandchildren. Our family owns and operates real estate businesses. However, all my adult life has been devoted to ministry. I earned degrees from theological institutions. I am a Christian. But since there are over 43,000 different kinds of Christian groups and denominations in the world the "Christian" designation won't help you understand me. (Someone told me there are over 40,000 different varieties of beans. Imagine that! There are more types of Christians than there are beans!) What differentiates me is my focus on love. I have been a hospital chaplain, pastor, counselor, teacher, trainer, workshop leader, vlogger, blogger and writer. This is my third book; all are about love. I hope to meet you someday. Maybe we can do a little hiking in Yosemite.